Scholastic BookFiles™

Island of the Blue Dolphins

by Scott O'Dell

Patricia McHugh

SCHOLASTIC
REFERENCE

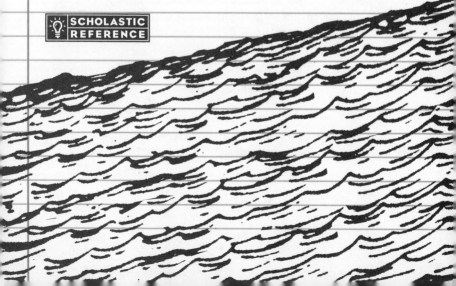

Library of Congress Cataloging-in-Publication Data

McHugh, Patricia, 1954–

Scholastic BookFiles: A Reading Guide to Island of the Blue Dolphins by Scott O'Dell/Patricia McHugh.

p.   cm.

Summary: Discusses the writing, characters, plot, and themes of this 1961 Newbery Award–winning book.

Includes discussion questions and activities.

Includes bibliographical references.

1. O'Dell, Scott, 1898–1989. Island of the Blue Dolphins—Juvenile literature.   2. California—In literature—Juvenile literature.   3. Survival in literature—Juvenile literature.   4. Solitude in literature—Juvenile literature.   5. Indians in literature—Juvenile literature.   6. Islands in literature—Juvenile literature.

[1. O'Dell, Scott, 1898–1989. Island of the Blue Dolphins.

2. American literature—History and criticism.]   I. Title.

PS3529.D434 I836 2003

813'.6—dc21   2002042489

0-439-46369-6

10 9 8 7 6 5 4 3   03 04 05 06 07

Composition by Brad Walrod/High Text Graphics, Inc.

Cover and interior design by Red Herring Design

Printed in the U.S.A.   23

First printing, July 2003

Contents

"Always, I knew I would be a writer."

–Scott O'Dell

When Scott O'Dell was born in Los Angeles on May 23, 1898, it was not the busy city it is today. "Los Angeles was a frontier town when I was born there," O'Dell said. "It had more horses than automobiles and more jackrabbits than people. The first sound I remember was a wildcat scratching on the roof of our house."

O'Dell grew up in California with his mother and father and a younger sister, Lucile. Because O'Dell's father worked for the railroad, the family moved often. They settled for a few years in the seaside town of San Pedro, California, and later lived in Julian, California, near the Mexican border. For a while, the family even lived on an island—Rattlesnake Island, near San Pedro. Their house was built on stilts, and when the tide came in, the seawater would wash under the house.

Wherever the family moved, though, they were never far from the Pacific Ocean or Los Angeles. "That is why, I suppose," said O'Dell, "the sound of the sea and the feel of the frontier are in my books." Many of O'Dell's experiences on the California coast later became part of Karana's story in *Island of the Blue Dolphins.*

Scott O'Dell was not the name the author was given at birth. In fact, it was quite the opposite: He was named Odell Scott! When he was a young adult, a typesetter accidentally switched the two words. O'Dell decided that he liked the new name better and legally changed his name.

O'Dell started school in a one-room schoolhouse, then attended other, larger schools as his family moved from place to place. He always liked to read. When O'Dell was still in elementary school, his parents told him that he was related to Sir Walter Scott, the well-known Scottish novelist. O'Dell was so impressed that he decided to become a writer himself when he grew up.

During high school, O'Dell was a track star. He graduated from Polytechnic High School in Long Beach, California. School came so easily to him that he never studied very hard. When he went to college, he found that he did not know how to focus on his studies. That's why, he once said, he wandered from college to college. He studied only what interested him—history, literature, philosophy, and psychology—and never earned a college degree.

O'Dell's first job was reading movie scripts in Hollywood. Then he worked in the movie business as a set dresser—preparing movie sets for different scenes—and as a camera operator. Later he supported himself as a writer and editor for newspapers and magazines. All the while, he was writing books for adults. He wrote seven altogether, including novels, a guidebook to Southern California, and a book about children's art.

During both World War I and World War II, O'Dell was a soldier, though he never actually fought in either war. He was still in training when World War I ended, and he was stationed in the United States during World War II.

O'Dell lived for many years in California, where he loved to sail and fish. For a while, he owned a sailboat that he sailed up and down the western coast of North America between Alaska and Mexico. O'Dell was married twice, the second time to Elizabeth Hall. He became a stepfather to Hall's two children from her previous marriage.

When O'Dell wrote *Island of the Blue Dolphins*, his first children's book, he was already in his early sixties. At a point in life when many people's careers are winding down, he was just beginning a second career as a children's book author. It was a career that would quickly bring him praise from around the world.

Island of the Blue Dolphins was published in 1960 and was awarded the 1961 Newbery Medal. The Newbery Medal is awarded each year by the American Library Association to the author of the most distinguished American children's book published the previous year. Earning this award for his first children's book was a great honor for O'Dell.

Six years after *Island of the Blue Dolphins* came out, O'Dell published his second children's book, *The King's Fifth*. The next year his third, *The Black Pearl*, appeared. *The King's Fifth* and *The Black Pearl* were both named Newbery Honor books. Newbery Honor awards are given to books that the Newbery committee thinks are excellent but that did not win the main Newbery Medal. O'Dell received a third Newbery Honor in 1971 for *Sing Down the Moon*.

After *Island of the Blue Dolphins*, O'Dell never wrote another adult book. He wrote a total of twenty-six children's books and began two more that his wife, Elizabeth Hall, finished after his death.

Most of O'Dell's children's books are works of historical fiction, novels that are part historical fact and part fiction. One of them, called *Zia*, is a story told by Karana's fictional niece, Zia. It reveals what happens to Karana after she leaves the Island of the Blue Dolphins.

In 1972, O'Dell was given the Hans Christian Andersen Award, the highest international award granted to an author or illustrator. Given every other year, the award honors one author and one illustrator "whose complete works have made a lasting contribution to children's literature."

After living most of his life on the West Coast, O'Dell moved to the East Coast in 1975. His wife had accepted a job in New York, and they moved to Westchester County, north of New York City. There, they bought a home on a lake. When he was not writing, O'Dell liked to plant trees and grow vegetables. He also pursued his lifelong passions for traveling, sailing, and fishing.

In 1982, O'Dell began a project to encourage others to write about history. He established the Scott O'Dell Award for Historical Fiction. Each year since 1984 this annual award of $5,000 has been given to the author of the best book of historical fiction for children.

O'Dell died of cancer on October 15, 1989. He was ninety-one years old. Although he died on the East Coast, his ashes were scattered in the sea off the coast of La Jolla, California. After the ceremony, as the mourners' boat turned back toward shore, a group of dolphins leaped from the water. The dolphins never left the boat's side until it turned from the ocean into the San Diego Bay.

How *Island of the Blue Dolphins* Came About

"I have a sincere feeling that I am able to say something to children, that someone is listening. I am not just entertaining them; I hope somewhere in each of my books there is something they will take away from it that is important to them as a person."

—Scott O'Dell

Scott O'Dell based *Island of the Blue Dolphins* on the history of a real person, but facts about her life were just part of the story. The rest he wrote from his imagination, inspired by many of his own experiences.

Island of the Blue Dolphins is based on the story of the Lost Woman of San Nicolas Island. She lived alone on San Nicolas for eighteen years, from 1835 to 1853, before being rescued and brought to the mainland. O'Dell tells some of her story in the Author's Note at the end of the novel.

In the early 1800s, the Indians of San Nicolas were fighting with Russian and Aleut sea otter hunters. The Aleuts were natives of the Aleutian Islands that lie off the mainland of Alaska.

San Nicolas Island lies off the coast of what is now called California. When the Lost Woman was left behind in 1835, this land belonged to Mexico. At that time, the California region was inhabited mostly by Native Americans and by missionaries. The missionaries were there to settle the land and teach the Native Americans about Christianity. Up and down the coast of California, the missionaries had developed small communities, called missions.

When the missionaries heard that hunters were threatening the islanders of San Nicolas, the missionaries offered to bring them to live at the Santa Barbara Mission. The islanders agreed, and in 1835, the missionaries sent a ship to bring them to the mainland. As the ship was leaving the island in bad weather, a young woman said that a child had been left behind. The other people on the boat refused to turn back. The young woman leaped from the boat and swam to shore. Eighteen years later, she was discovered still alive on the island, dressed in a skirt of cormorant feathers and accompanied by a dog.

By the time the Lost Woman was rescued, all traces of her tribe had disappeared. No one could be found who spoke her language, so she could not tell people much about her experiences alone on the island. She died just seven weeks after coming to the mission, probably because she could not adjust to her new diet. The people at the mission, who never learned her real name, gave her the Christian name Juana Maria and buried her at the mission.

O'Dell knew the Lost Woman's story for many years before he began to write about it. He first heard her story when he read a short magazine article about her in 1920. He found the story interesting but did nothing with it. As the years passed, he sometimes came across other mentions of the story. What finally inspired him to write about the Lost Woman? Hunters did.

In the late 1950s, O'Dell was living in the mountains of California near Mexico. He was not sure what he wanted to write about next. But he did know that he was angry at the hunters who were killing many animals in the mountains. He became so angry that he began to hate them. He wrote, "That hatred combined itself with the memory of this legend about the girl on the island, eighteen years alone . . . and it became an idea, not for a book, exactly, but just something that I wanted to say—really, to myself—and to sort this out."

O'Dell had two important pieces of his story: It would be a survival story based on the Lost Woman's history, and it would be a protest against the senseless killing of animals. But how would he bring the Lost Woman, whom he now called Karana, to life?

He found much of what he needed in experiences from his own life.

O'Dell knew the Channel Islands and the coast of California from his many experiences there as a child and as an adult. As a boy, O'Dell had hunted for devilfish along the rocky coast with his friends. Another childhood adventure became the basis for Karana's journey by canoe. O'Dell once described his adventure this way: "Many summer days we left the landlocked world and went to sea. How? Each of us on a separate log. The logs had been towed into the harbor in great rafts—from Oregon. They were twelve feet long or longer, rough with splinters and covered with tar." They might have been just logs, but to O'Dell and his friends, "they were proud canoes."

Some details of Karana's character were inspired by a Mexican girl whom O'Dell and his wife had met. She was a sixteen-year-old named Carolina, a strong, straightforward girl who "stood in her bare feet squarely on the earth as if growing from it." She was always careful to share the O'Dells' gifts with her brothers and sisters, showing the same loving spirit that Karana later showed to Ramo. Carolina also had a skirt that she treasured, much as Karana loved her skirt of cormorant feathers. "The two girls are much alike," O'Dell once said.

O'Dell loved dogs and knew how to describe a close relationship with one. He once had a German shepherd named Eric that went everywhere with him. In fact, O'Dell would only stay at hotels that welcomed the dog. When Eric became sick with his final illness, O'Dell nursed him sadly, fanning him through a long, hot summer. He once spoke about Eric's death in a way that sounds very much like Rontu's death: "Slowly, he walked to where I was standing and fell at my feet. I put my hand on his chest. I could feel his heart beating, very slowly . . . and then no more."

When he wrote *Island of the Blue Dolphins*, O'Dell also used memories of behavior he was less than proud of. As a child he had sometimes killed wild animals out of curiosity. When he grew up, he was always horrified to remember what he had done, and he was determined to help other people learn to treat animals properly.

O'Dell had an enemy as a child, much as Karana has enemies in the wild dogs and the Aleuts. O'Dell's enemy was a bully, a boy who tormented him both in and out of school. When O'Dell and his childhood enemy met later as adults, O'Dell was prepared to hate him still. He found he couldn't—and he used that feeling of forgiveness to show how Karana could befriend two members of enemy groups: Rontu, a wild dog, and Tutok, an Aleut.

After O'Dell wrote *Island of the Blue Dolphins*, he showed it to a friend, children's book author Maud Lovelace. To his surprise, she told him that he had written his first children's book. O'Dell once said, "I didn't know what young people were reading and I didn't consider [*Island of the Blue Dolphins*] a children's book, necessarily."

O'Dell's editor agreed to publish *Island of the Blue Dolphins* soon after he submitted it. The book quickly became one of the best-loved children's books ever written.

Chapter Charter: Questions to Guide Your Reading

T he following questions will help you think about the important parts of each chapter.

Chapter 1
- Do you think that Karana is a responsible person? What about Ramo? How much do you think their ages affect whether or not they are responsible?
- How would you describe the relationship between the islanders and the Aleuts as the story begins?

Chapter 2
- What do the islanders do that contributes to bad feelings between them and the Aleuts?

Chapter 3
- Why might Karana's people need to know exactly when the hunters will leave?

Chapter 4
- If Chief Chowig had not argued with the hunters about payment, what do you think would have happened that day? What might have happened the next time the hunters came to the island?

Chapter 5

- Why do you think Kimki decides that the tribe should leave the island?

Chapter 6

- Why do you think Nanko teases the islanders instead of telling them the good news right away? Can you think of a time when you've done that?

Chapter 7

- The islanders are leaving their home forever on a strange ship. How might you feel if you had to move away from your home? Is there one special thing you would never leave behind, as Ramo will not leave his spear?
- Both Chief Matasaip and Karana have to make difficult decisions about going back for Ramo. The chief decides not to turn back; Karana decides to do so. Do you think either person made the right decision? What would you have done?

Chapter 8

- After Ramo dies, Karana vows to kill all of the wild dogs on the island. Does this seem fair to you?

Chapter 9

- Why do you think Karana burns down the village of Ghalas-at? Would you have made the same decision? Why or why not?
- Karana decides to disobey the law that forbids women from making weapons. Can you think of a situation in which you might have to disobey a law to save your life?

Chapter 10
- Karana undertakes a dangerous journey when she leaves the island by canoe. Why do you think she feels desperate enough to risk her life this way?

Chapter 11
- Why do you think Karana decides that she will never again leave the island unless the white men come for her?
- As Karana chooses a location for her new home, what are some of the issues she has to consider? Do you think she chooses wisely?

Chapter 12
- As Karana builds her new home, how does she protect herself from animals and from the weather? Why do you think she tries to make her life more comfortable?

Chapter 13
- Karana sees two large male sea elephants fighting. Do you think the younger or the older animal will win? Why?

Chapter 14
- What do you think is different about Karana's second home, compared with her first?

Chapter 15
- Why does Karana decide she must kill the leader of the dog pack? What changes her mind?
- Why do you think the leader of the dog pack begins to trust her, rather than wants to harm her?

Chapter 16

- Karana's life changes after she befriends Rontu. Have you ever had a pet or a human friend who has changed your life? If so, can you describe how?

Chapter 17

- When Rontu goes back to the wild dogs, Karana doesn't help him fight. Have you ever had a pet that needed your help? If so, what happened? Were you able to help it?

Chapter 18

- In this chapter, Karana describes a spring season when she is especially happy. Would you have been happy in her situation during that spring?

Chapter 19

- Why does Karana want to spear the devilfish? Why do you think she later decides never to hunt one again?

Chapter 20

- As Karana explores Black Cave, what does she discover there? How does it make her feel? If you were Karana, would you ever return to Black Cave? Why or why not?
- When the Aleuts come, what does Karana do to hide from them?

Chapter 21

- Do you think Karana is more afraid of the Aleut girl or of the hunters?

- Do you think that the Aleut girl is afraid of Karana? Why or why not?

Chapter 22

- How do we know that Karana has come to trust Tutok?
- Why do you think Karana cooks food for Tutok even though she knows Tutok is gone?

Chapter 23

- What does it mean that Karana eventually gives the otter a name, Mon-a-nee?
- Why do you think the otter did not stay in the pool?

Chapter 24

- As time passes, Karana's feelings about killing animals change. How did she once feel, and how does she feel now? Why do you think her feelings change?

Chapter 25

- Karana loses her best friend when Rontu dies. Describe how it might feel to lose a favorite animal.

Chapter 26

- Why do you think Karana tries to catch the wild dog that is Rontu's son?

Chapter 27

- Before the earthquake, what are some of the signs Karana notices that something abnormal is happening to the sea and to the island?

Chapter 28

- The author almost never uses words that describe how Karana is feeling. We can often guess, though, by how he describes what Karana is doing. From his descriptions, what do you think Karana is feeling when she first sees the ship? when she realizes that she doesn't know whose ship it is? when she hears the man calling her? when she realizes that the ship has left without her?

Chapter 29

- The white men want Karana to change into clothes like theirs. Why do you think they do this?
- Do you think Karana will have a better life after she leaves the island? What might her life be like?

"I walked across the deck and, though many hands tried to hold me back, flung myself into the sea."

—Karana, *Island of the Blue Dolphins*

Island of the Blue Dolphins is the story of Karana, an American Indian girl who survives alone on an island for many years.

Twelve-year-old Karana lives in the village of Ghalas-at on the Island of the Blue Dolphins. One day Karana and her six-year-old brother, Ramo, see a ship sailing toward their island. Karana is excited but uneasy.

The men of Ghalas-at race to meet the ship. Forty Aleuts and their Russian captain, named Orlov, have come to hunt sea otters. Orlov says that they will pay the islanders with jewelry and metal spearheads. Karana's father, Chief Chowig, does not trust the hunters. Still, he agrees to let them hunt. Karana's sister, Ulape, declares that one of the Aleuts is a girl, but no one believes her.

When the Aleuts are done hunting, they argue with the islanders about payment. The Aleuts and the islanders fight on the beach, and many island men die. The tribe is devastated. "There was no woman who had not lost a father or a husband, a brother or a son."

The new tribal chief, Kimki, travels across the sea to find a new place for the tribe. After he leaves, Matasaip becomes chief.

A year later, another ship sails into the harbor. Kimki has sent the white men and their ship to bring the tribe to their new home.

A storm is coming, so the islanders hurry to board the ship. Ramo has forgotten his treasured fishing spear and wants to go back for it. Karana says no, but Ramo disobeys her. As the ship sails out to sea, Karana sees Ramo alone on the island. She begs Chief Matasaip to go back for him. "We cannot wait for Ramo," he says. "If we do, the ship will be driven on the rocks." The chief promises to come back for him on another trip. "He will be safe," he says.

Karana does not believe him. She dives back into the sea and swims to shore. She hugs Ramo and promises that they will be rescued soon.

Sadly, there will be no rescue for Ramo, who is soon killed by wild dogs. Karana vows that someday she will kill the dogs that killed her brother.

After Ramo's death, Karana decides that she can no longer live in the village of empty huts that remind her "of all the people who were dead and those who were gone." She burns each house in the village until "there were only ashes left to mark the village of Ghalas-at."

Karana makes a new home on a large rock. There she is safe from the dogs, though they follow her when she leaves the rock. She needs weapons to kill the dogs but she is afraid to disobey her tribe's law, which states that women are not allowed to make weapons.

Karana looks everywhere for weapons but finds none. She decides that she must disobey the tribe's law. She makes a spear and then a bow and arrows. Feeling more secure with her weapons nearby, Karana begins to enjoy her new life. Still, she waits for the ship to return for her and always "at dawn, as light spread across the sea, my first glance was toward the little harbor of Coral Cove."

After the dogs threaten her again, Karana decides to leave the island by canoe. She is not really afraid, she says, for whatever might happen to her means "far less than the thought of staying on the island alone, without a home or companions, pursued by wild dogs, where everything reminded me of those who were dead and those who had gone away."

Karana paddles out to sea, but the old canoe is leaking and starts to split apart. Karana realizes that she must turn back to the island, though she is uncertain if she will make it. When a swarm of dolphins swims near her canoe, they lift her spirits and give her the strength to paddle home.

Grateful to be alive, Karana settles into life on the island. She builds a home on the headland and furnishes it. She makes new, stronger weapons to hunt the wild dogs. She plans to kill a sea elephant for its sharp teeth, which she can use as spear points. Instead, she witnesses a terrible fight between two sea elephants that leads to one of the sea elephants' death.

Karana stumbles and badly injures her leg as she watches the fight. She hides from the wild dogs in a cave and, after she recovers, makes it into a second shelter.

Karana makes spear points from the teeth of the dead sea elephant and hunts the wild dogs. She wounds the leader of the pack, a big dog that she thinks must have come with the Aleuts. When she follows the wounded dog into the brush, she is surprised to find that she does not want to kill him, though she is not sure why. She nurses the dog back to health and, when he is better, names him Rontu.

Next, Karana decides to fix one of the tribe's old canoes. As she does so, Rontu plays nearby. Now Karana realizes how lonely she had been before she "had Rontu to talk to." Karana and Rontu use the canoe to explore the island's caves, where they hunt a giant devilfish and find ancient figures her ancestors once made.

Then one day the Aleuts return. This time, Karana sees for herself that they have a girl with them. Though Karana hides, the Aleut girl discovers her. Slowly the two become friends.

The girls visit together for many days before the Aleuts leave. Afterward, Karana listens to the many familiar sounds of the island. "But suddenly," she says to herself, "as I thought of Tutok, the island seemed very quiet."

Karana goes down to the beach and sees the dead and dying otters the Aleuts have left behind. She is able to save one otter, who becomes her friend Mon-a-nee. As time passes, her pet birds, Tainor and Lurai, have two baby birds, and Karana nurses an injured young gull. Karana decides that she will never kill another otter, cormorant, seal, dog, or sea elephant again. Even if her tribespeople were to come back and laugh at her, she would not change her mind.

Rontu dies, but Karana soon catches and tames a wild dog that is Rontu's son and names him Rontu-Aru.

Karana barely survives an earthquake that strikes first at sea and then on the island. She loses all her food, weapons, and canoes. As she is piecing together a new canoe on the beach one day, she sees a ship on the horizon. Karana hides, not knowing at first if the men on board are dangerous Aleuts or rescuers. By the time she realizes they are rescuers, the men have left. She is alone again on the island.

Two years later, the same ship returns. Karana knows that this time she will leave on the ship. She carefully prepares, dressing in her finest clothes and jewelry. The white men greet Karana in a strange language. Though she doesn't understand what they are saying, the words are sweet to her. "They were the sound of a human voice. There is no sound like this in all the world."

As the ship sails for the mainland, Karana says to the reader, "For a long time I stood and looked back at the Island of the Blue Dolphins." She thinks of all the animals she has left behind "and of all the happy days." Dolphins accompany the ship far out to sea. Her little birds chirp and Rontu-Aru sits beside Karana as she sails toward her new life.

Thinking about the plot
• Why do the islanders and the Aleuts fight?
• How does Karana become stranded on the Island of the Blue Dolphins?
• What are the greatest dangers Karana faces, and how does she respond to them?
• How is Karana rescued?

"The Island of the Blue Dolphins was
my home; I had no other. It would be
my home until the white men returned
in their ship."

—Karana, *Island of the Blue Dolphins*

Island of the Blue Dolphins takes place entirely on the island and in the nearby ocean during the mid-1800s.

Time

Although O'Dell never mentions any dates in *Island of the Blue Dolphins*, we know the general time period since the novel is based on a true story. The real Lost Woman of San Nicolas lived alone on the island for eighteen years, between 1835 and 1853. Certain details of the story show us that O'Dell kept his novel in the same time period.

We see that the story takes place when the islanders are just beginning to be affected by outside cultures. Hunters have been to the Island of the Blue Dolphins only once before in the islanders' memory. Also, the white men helping the islanders are missionaries from the Santa Barbara Mission. Missions were the main white settlements in California from the late 1700s to the mid-1800s. The hunters and the white men arrive in sailing ships of the sort that were used a hundred years or more ago. The Aleuts and the Russians have tools and objects that are almost as simple as the ones the Indians use: They fish for otters with spears, and as payment they offer beads and iron spearheads.

A number of years pass during the course of the book. The author shows this by letting whole seasons or years go by with a simple comment such as, "For many summers after the Aleuts had gone..." or "After two more springs had gone..." He also gives us a dramatic sense that many years have passed when he describes how Karana has marked the passage of time. For a long time, Karana counts the passing moons (months) by making a mark for each on a pole by her door. So much time passes that "there were many marks, from the roof to the floor." After a while, though, she stops marking the moons and begins marking only the four seasons. Finally, during the last year when she doubts that she will ever be rescued, she does not mark the passing time at all.

Place

The author creates the island setting by weaving details into nearly every paragraph in the book. O'Dell describes the island itself and the many creatures that live on or near it. He gives us many details of the Indians' culture, as well as some details about the cultures of the Aleuts and the white men. He also uses language to help make the setting real.

The island in the title of the book is based on the real island of San Nicolas. San Nicolas is one of the Channel Islands that lie off the coast of California, southwest of Santa Barbara and Los Angeles. Just as O'Dell describes it in the novel, San Nicolas was once home to American Indians and was a hunting place for the Aleuts and the Russians who came in search of sea otters. The island is now used by the U.S. Navy, and the public is not allowed to visit.

O'Dell loved the ocean and island life. He had lived near the sea for many years and had lived on an island for part of his childhood. So he knew many details of island life and used them to help establish the setting.

O'Dell describes the island in such detail that it is possible to draw a map from his descriptions. Karana gives us an overall picture:

> Our island is two leagues long and one league wide, and if you were standing on one of the hills that rise in the middle of it, you would think that it looked like a fish. Like a dolphin lying on its side, with its tail pointing toward the sunrise, its nose pointing to the sunset, and its fins making reefs and the rocky ledges along the shore. [A league is about three miles long, or five kilometers.]

The author uses vivid details to help us visualize the island setting. Right from the beginning of the story he gives us details such as these: The ship sails around the *kelp bed* and between two *large rocks* that guard *Coral Cove*. The men race down the *trail* to the *shore;* the women gather on the *mesa.* Karana moves through *heavy brush* and down the *ravine* to the *sea cliffs,* where she hides in the *toyon bushes.*

O'Dell describes other aspects of the environment, from the island's constant wind and the motion of the sea to descriptions of the changing seasons and of a frightening earthquake.

The characters in *Island of the Blue Dolphins* act and speak in ways that show they are living in and have a deep understanding of their natural environment. As the story begins, they are digging for roots to eat. From a distance, the ship looks like a shell to Karana, then a gull with folded wings. Ramo guesses that it is a cloud or a whale, then a very large canoe. Karana compares Ramo with a cricket, and thinks his eyes are like lizards' eyes. Karana and Ramo also talk about some of the animals on their island, the dolphins, gulls, cormorants, otters, and whales. We are immediately as immersed in their island world as they are.

As the story unfolds, we can see island life through its many other creatures, too, from wild dogs, sea elephants, and devilfish to red foxes, sea gulls, and pelicans.

O'Dell uses his knowledge of Channel Island Indian culture to make his setting seem real. Because of his careful research, O'Dell knew a great deal about how the native people lived. He describes the Indian village and the things that the islanders made and used, from their houses to their clothing, tools, and weapons. He shows us what they ate and how they prepared their food. Though O'Dell does not go into such detail about the Aleuts and the white men, he tells us enough about their appearance, equipment, and habits to make them seem real.

The author uses language to help involve us in island life. Karana tells the story using simple words and ideas that show us she has little knowledge of the world beyond the island. O'Dell introduces some words in the characters' native languages, too. We find out several of the islanders' everyday names and their real, but secret, names. We also learn some of the Aleuts' words as well as those of the islanders. Sometimes we can compare them. For instance, we see that the Aleut word for "pretty"—*wintscha*—is similar to the islanders' word for "pretty"—*win-tai.* Using similar words is also a way for O'Dell to say that different groups of people are not really so different from one another, after all.

Thinking about the setting
• Describe the setting of *Island of the Blue Dolphins.*
• How does the author use language to establish the setting?
• When does *Island of the Blue Dolphins* take place?

"I tried to convey a simple, but profound, message: Forgive your enemies and have respect for life— all life."

—Scott O'Dell

Scott O'Dell often said that the two most important themes of *Island of the Blue Dolphins* were forgiveness and respect for all life. The book has other themes, too, including the themes of survival and of the place of girls and women in society.

Forgiveness

O'Dell wanted to show people how important he thought it was to get along with others and to forgive your enemies.

The first enemy Karana forgives is not a person, but a dog. Rontu is an enemy because he is the leader of the dog pack that kills Ramo and threatens Karana. He is also an enemy because he is an Aleut dog, and the Aleuts are Karana's enemies.

After Ramo dies, Karana vows that "some day I would go back and kill the wild dogs in the cave. I would kill all of them." This is a promise of revenge as much as one of self-defense. She wants to kill them not only to punish them for killing Ramo but also because they threaten her.

Karana kills some of the dogs with the weapons she makes. She decides that she has to be sure to kill the leader, because he has made the pack bolder and more dangerous.

Karana wounds Rontu, but she finds that she is reluctant to kill him. She says, "Why I did not send the arrow I cannot say. . . . The big dog lay there and did not move and this may be the reason. If he had gotten up I would have killed him."

Karana feeds the dog and nurses him back to health. She does this out of a sense of duty rather than because she cares about the dog. "I had no thought that he would live and I did not care."

As the days pass, Karana's caretaking of Rontu has an effect on them both: They begin to truly care about each other. When Karana returns with a fish for Rontu on the fourth day, she is relieved that he has not left. Rontu looks "first at the fish I carried and then at me and moved his tail." Soon Karana's worst enemy has become her first friend on the island since she was left alone.

Later, Karana has another chance to forgive and befriend an enemy—this time, an Aleut.

In the years before the story begins, the Aleuts had come to hunt on the Island of the Blue Dolphins and had treated the islanders poorly. Karana's tribespeople have distrusted the Aleuts ever since. When the Aleuts return at the beginning of the story, they cause bad feelings again by cheating the islanders. The two groups fight and many men die.

But when the Aleuts come to the island a third time, when Karana is alone there, Karana learns that an enemy can become a friend. This happens when she gets to know one Aleut, a girl named Tutok.

When Karana first sees Tutok, Karana almost attacks her with a spear. Karana surprises herself when she does not throw the spear at Tutok, "for she was one of the Aleuts who had killed my people on the beach of Coral Cove."

Though Tutok can see that Karana distrusts her, Tutok is friendly. She tells Karana her name and smiles at her. She touches Karana's cormorant skirt and holds it against her body. Karana admits to herself that the skirt looks nice on Tutok, but "I hated the Aleuts and took it from her."

Though Karana struggles to hold on to her hatred, it is weakening. She has not heard a human voice in so long that Tutok's words sound good to her, "even though it was an enemy who spoke them."

When Tutok gives Karana a beautiful necklace, Karana begins to see that Tutok could be her friend. Still, Karana does not trust Tutok completely. Only after two more days of visiting does Karana trust Tutok enough to tell Tutok her real, secret name. After that, the girls spend many days together. Karana has made a true friend—a well-earned reward for learning to forgive an enemy.

Respect for all life

When O'Dell wrote *Island of the Blue Dolphins* in the late 1950s, it was one of the first children's books to suggest that animals deserve to be treated with the same respect as people. O'Dell loved animals, though he did not always treat them well as a child. When he grew up he was ashamed of his behavior and wanted to help others learn to treat them properly.

Karana's tribespeople must hunt animals to survive. They depend on animals, especially fish, as food. They need animal skins to make clothing. They need animal bones, teeth, and sinews to make tools and shelters. When the Russian and the Aleut hunters come, they change the islanders' traditional relationship with animals. Now, animals are hunted for profit as well as to fulfill basic needs. Many more animals are killed, and because the hunters want only their skins, many otters' bodies lie wasted on the shore. The islanders approve of killing the otters because they, too, will share in the profits.

Though Karana kills animals to satisfy her needs, we see from the beginning of the story that her feelings about animals are already different from other islanders'. Karana is the only islander who worries that the hunters will kill too many otters. She sees these gentle, playful creatures as her friends.

Karana slowly becomes more and more sympathetic toward animals. She plans to kill a sea elephant for its sharp teeth, but instead she is injured as she watches a bloody battle between two sea elephants. Hunting begins to lose some of its appeal.

Karana has her first real change of heart about animals when she befriends Rontu. Now she begins to see some animals as individual creatures and potential friends. She soon makes pets of the birds Tainor and Lurai as well.

When Karana tries to kill the giant devilfish, it fights back hard, hurting both her and Rontu. Karana decides never to try to kill a devilfish again. She is beginning to respect even the animals that threaten her. Still, she then kills ten cormorants to make a feather skirt.

A turning point for Karana comes when the hunters return to the island after Karana has lived there alone for years. After the hunters finish their hunt and leave the island, Karana is disturbed to see the dead and dying sea otters they have left behind. She tries to undo some of the harm the hunters have done, killing the badly injured otters and nursing one back to health. Soon, she befriends the otter's pups and realizes that she can never harm another sea otter again. More than this, she realizes that she can never again harm a cormorant or a seal, a wild dog or a sea elephant. Her tribespeople would have laughed at her, she knows, but even then she would not have changed her mind, for "this is the way I felt about the animals who had become my friends and those who were not, but in time could be."

Karana must be practical, of course. She must still eat, and she does continue to catch fish and gather shellfish. The author doesn't discuss how Karana will satisfy her other needs. We can imagine how ourselves: She could, for instance, make use of animals that have already died, or she could substitute non-animal materials for the ones she would have taken from animals.

At the end of the story, the white men who rescue Karana ask her to show them where they can find otters to hunt. Karana will not do it. "I shook my head and acted as though I did not understand." Even though Karana is grateful that the men have rescued her, she will not repay them by helping them kill animals.

Survival

Another important theme of *Island of the Blue Dolphins* is survival. How will Karana survive alone on the island? Will she ever leave the island and live with other people again?

Karana has many skills because in her culture children are very involved in the tasks of daily living. She knows how to gather and prepare food and how to make clothing, for instance. But after Karana is left alone on the island, she must do many more things that adults once did for her. She has to make a shelter to protect herself from animals and the weather. She has to improvise tools, repair the canoes, and make weapons.

Karana also learns that survival means more than just keeping yourself alive. She must take care of her needs for friendship, comfort, and pleasure, too.

Because there are no other humans on the island, she makes friends with the animals, including Rontu, the sea otter Mon-a-nee, and the birds Tainor and Lurai. After Karana befriends Tutok, she realizes how much a human friend means to her, too.

To fulfill her needs for comfort and pleasure, Karana makes herself a comfortable and clean house. She sews herself a beautiful skirt from cormorant feathers and makes earrings to match the necklace that Tutok gives her.

Girls and women in society

Another theme is that of girls' and women's place in society. O'Dell admired girls and women, and felt that they did not always get the respect they deserved. To do something about this, he liked to make them important characters in his books. In many of his books, a girl is the main character. When O'Dell wrote about girls, he always portrayed them as strong, capable people.

In Karana's tribe, men and women usually do different work. The men hunt, fish, and build canoes. The women are "never asked to do more than stay at home, cook food, and make clothing." But after most of the young men are killed, the women begin to do the men's work, too. It turns out that they do the work well. "So hard did the women work that we really fared better than before when the hunting was done by the men."

But the men do not want to share their work with the women. The chief again forbids the women from hunting. If the tribe had not left the island soon after, this might have become another crisis.

Alone on the island, Karana struggles with her society's rules for women when she needs weapons to defend herself against the wild dogs. In her tribe, women are not allowed to make weapons. Karana asks herself what will happen if she breaks the law: "Would the four winds blow in from the four directions of the world and smother me as I made the weapons? Or would the earth tremble, as many said, and bury me beneath its falling rocks?..."

Despite her fear, Karana makes weapons and uses them. When she is not punished, Karana realizes that the law was unfair to women and that it made sense for her to disobey it.

Thinking about the themes
• What are the two main themes in the book, according to the author?
• What are some other themes in the book?
• Why do Karana's feelings about killing animals change?
• Why do Karana's feelings about enemies change? Do you consider any people or animals your enemies? Did your feelings about enemies change after you read the novel?

Characters: Who Are These People, Anyway?

There are a number of characters in the novel, although by chapter nine, most of them will no longer appear in the story. The main characters are Karana, Ramo, Rontu, and Tutok.

Here is a list of characters. Following that is a brief description of each of the main characters.

People

Karana	main character, twelve years old when the novel begins
Ramo	Karana's six-year-old brother
Chief Chowig	Karana's father
Ulape	Karana's fourteen-year-old sister
Captain Orlov	Russian captain in charge of the hunting ship
Aleuts	hunters who work for Orlov
Kimki	new chief after Chowig's death; he leaves the island by canoe
Matasaip	new chief after Kimki leaves
Nanko	island man whom Ulape loves
Tutok	Aleut girl who befriends Karana

| white men | men who come to take the islanders to the mainland |
| Father Gonzales | missionary Karana meets after she leaves the island |

Animals

Rontu	dog that Karana tames
Tainor and Lurai	birds that Karana tames
Mon-a-nee	otter that Karana helps (later called Won-a-nee)
Rontu-Aru	Rontu's son

Karana: Karana, the main character in the book, is a twelve-year-old girl at the beginning of the novel. She is responsible, loving, and brave. She likes animals and pretty things. She considers the Aleuts and the wild dogs her enemies. As time passes, Karana changes in important ways. She learns that sometimes she has to disobey the rules. She comes to care deeply about animals. And she befriends two former enemies.

Karana is always a responsible girl. Like the other children on the island, Karana has important work to do, and she takes it seriously. At the beginning of the story she is taking care of her brother, Ramo, while gathering food for the tribe. She takes good care of Ramo. Even though he is annoying her, she is patient and cheerful. And though she wants to run off to see the ship coming into the cove, she goes on digging roots until her basket is full, "because they were needed in the village." Only when she finishes her work does she go to see the excitement in the cove.

After her father and many other island men die, Karana must become even more responsible. She works harder than ever for the tribe and struggles to care for Ramo without her father's help.

Later in the story, Karana still wants to do what is expected of her, but she eventually does something that her tribe would not approve of. She disobeys the law that women cannot make weapons. She decides that it is more important for her to survive than to obey this law.

Karana is brave. She first proves her bravery when she dives back into the sea to go back to Ramo, knowing that he will be frightened and in danger alone on the island. Karana will have many more chances to show her bravery, from fighting the wild dogs to trying to cross the sea alone in a canoe.

We also know that Karana likes animals, even at the beginning of the story when she is still willing to kill them. When she sees the Aleuts killing so many sea otters, she is angry, "for these animals were my friends." Her father laughs at her "foolishness," and so we learn that she is more sensitive to animals than others in her tribe. Karana's love of animals becomes even stronger as she comes to know them better. By the end of the story, she decides that she will never again kill an animal unless she must do so for her own survival.

After Karana's tribesmen are killed by Aleuts and her brother is killed by wild dogs, Karana decides that the Aleuts and the wild dogs are her enemies. She is afraid of them and willing to injure or even kill them to protect herself. Later, after she befriends the dog, Rontu, and the Aleut, Tutok, she realizes that enemies can be forgiven and can become friends.

Karana loves pretty clothes and jewelry, and sometimes dresses up just for herself. When the tribe leaves the island, she is told to take only necessary things. But she cannot stop herself from packing her skirt of yucca fiber, "for I had spent many days making it and it was very pretty." As she hides from the Aleuts in the cave, she passes her time making a skirt of cormorant feathers. Finally, when the ship comes to take her from the island, she wears her most beautiful clothes and jewelry and decorates her face with the tribal marks that show she is unmarried.

Ramo: Ramo is Karana's six-year-old brother. He is small for his age, but "quick as a cricket." Ramo is smart and observant, too. When he sees a ship for the first time, he has no idea what it is. Suddenly he realizes that it must be something like an enormous canoe and shouts, "A great one, bigger than all of our canoes together. And red!"

Ramo is also "foolish as a cricket" when he is excited. He forgets all about his work collecting roots and rushes off as soon as he sees the ship. He "tossed the root in the air and was gone, crashing through the brush, shouting as he went."

When the boat comes to take the Indians from the island, Ramo, excitable as ever, "hopped along far in front with one of our baskets." But "before long he ran back to say that he had forgotten his fishing spear." Karana refuses to let him get his spear. Ramo disobeys her, and the ship leaves without him.

Even after he and Karana are abandoned on the island, Ramo is still excited. He thinks it will be fun to be alone with Karana. He does not realize that he has put them both in danger. He brags that he is now chief of the island. He says that he is strong enough to bring a canoe to the cove and sneaks off to do so. This final, unwise adventure leads to his death. While traveling to the place where the canoes are hidden, Ramo is attacked by wild dogs and killed.

Rontu: Rontu is the leader of the pack of wild dogs that kill Ramo. Karana first sees him as she carries Ramo's body back to the village. The dog is "a big gray dog with long curling hair and yellow eyes." He has thick fur around his neck. Because Karana had never seen him before the Aleuts came, she guesses that he is an Aleut dog. The dog is much larger than the native dogs, which all have short hair and brown eyes. Karana thinks that the pack has grown even bolder since the Aleut dog became their leader.

The dog pack threatens Karana many times. Since the Aleut dog is their leader, Karana decides that she must kill him. Still, Karana sometimes sees him watching her quietly, and her special awareness of him lets us know that he will be important to the story.

When Karana finally aims an arrow at him, he is not frightened. Rather than running away, he faces her bravely, "his front legs spread as if he were ready to spring, his yellow eyes narrowed to slits." After Karana strikes him with an arrow, he runs off into the brush.

When Karana finds him again, he is too weak to defend himself. She takes him home and cares for him. At first he is so weak that he does not respond to her at all. Later, he growls when she holds out her hand to him. Finally, as he begins to recover, he wags his tail at her. Karana names him Rontu, and they become friends.

Tutok: Tutok is an Aleut girl who comes with the hunters on both of their trips to the island. During the first trip, we learn very little about Tutok. In fact, Ulape is the only one who sees her. Ulape says that the girl "is dressed in skins just like the men. But she wears a fur cap and under the cap she has thick hair that falls to her waist." None of the other islanders believe that Tutok even exists. But when the Aleuts return on their second trip, Tutok is with them again, as Karana sees for herself.

Soon, Tutok discovers Karana. Tutok is a warm, friendly girl. She agrees with Karana that Rontu is now Karana's dog rather than her own. She tells Karana her name and admires Karana's skirt. Tutok brings Karana a beautiful necklace of black stones. Karana slowly begins to trust Tutok, and finally they become friends.

Tutok visits many times before the Aleuts leave the island. Tutok never returns, but Karana does not forget her or her kindness.

Thinking about the characters

- Is Karana like other twelve-year-olds you know? Do you like or admire her? When she is older, how has she changed?
- How would you describe Ramo? Does he seem like a typical six-year-old? Is he someone you would like or admire?
- Why do you think Ramo adapts so easily to being Karana's dog, after being a wild dog?
- If Tutok had been a less friendly person, what might have happened when she and Karana met?

It's an award winner!

Winning the Newbery Medal for *Island of the Blue Dolphins* was a great honor for Scott O'Dell. The Newbery Medal was the first and most important award the book won, but it was not the only one. Since then, *Island of the Blue Dolphins* has won at least twelve other awards from national and international groups.

Book critics loved the book, too. A writer for *The New York Times* called it "haunting" and said that O'Dell's writing style was "beautifully fitted to his subject." A critic writing in *The Times* of London called it "a novel of the highest excellence."

But as exciting as it was to have adults praise his work, O'Dell was also pleased that children loved his book. *Island of the Blue Dolphins* has been read by children all around the world, and has been translated into at least twenty-three languages.

Is this a true story?

This kind of question often comes up with a work of historical fiction. How is the reader to know what is fact and what is fiction? Sometimes the reader can only find out by learning more about the historical time described. Often, though, the author will include a section that helps explain what is real and what comes from his imagination, as O'Dell does in his Author's Note at the end of *Island of the Blue Dolphins.*

Scott O'Dell used even more facts than the ones he mentions in his Author's Note. For instance, many details about the islanders' everyday lives came from facts about the real Channel Island Indians.

What we consider to be the "facts" of history sometimes changes over time, too. Since O'Dell wrote *Island of the Blue Dolphins,* a number of researchers have questioned certain facts about the Lost Woman's life. For instance, some think that she might have been in her twenties when she was left behind and that the child she went back for was her son, not her brother. Nevertheless, O'Dell used the facts as he understood them at the time. From the information he had, he wrote a powerful story that realistically describes what it must have been like for a young woman to be left alone on an island for eighteen years.

Is the story too sad for children?

Many sad things happen in *Island of the Blue Dolphins,* from the deaths of Chowig, Ramo, and the other tribespeople to Karana's loss of Rontu, Tutok, and, finally, her island home. Is this too much sadness in a story for children? Some people think so. Others say that the sadness is brightened by Karana's brave spirit, her exciting adventures, and her final success in leaving the island to be with other people again.

Thinking about what others think about
Island of the Blue Dolphins

- Why do you think *Island of the Blue Dolphins* has won so many awards? What makes it special? Did you like it as much as other people seem to like it?
- Do you like historical fiction? When you read historical fiction, do you want to know which part is fact and which part is fiction?
- Overall, did the novel seem too sad to you? Or were only some parts of the novel too sad? If so, which ones?

bales large bundles tied tightly together

brush land covered with shrubs and short trees

canyon a deep narrow valley with steep sides

carcass a dead body of an animal

cove a small sheltered bay or inlet along a coast

crevice a crack or split in something

fledglings young birds

gruel a thin meal made by cooking food in water; watery porridge

headland a point of land high above the sea

kelp large brown seaweed

lair a place where wild animals live and rest

league a measure of distance, about three miles (five kilometers)

lure an attraction

mesa a steep hill with a flat top

omen a sign or warning about something that will happen in the future

paces footsteps used to measure distance

parley to discuss something you disagree about

pelt an animal skin with the fur or hair still attached

pitch a dark, sticky substance made from wood or other materials

planks thick wooden boards

ponder to think carefully about

ravine a deep, narrow valley that is smaller than a canyon

rites acts done for a ceremony

shirkers people who avoid doing what they should do

shrouded covered

sinews tough cords of tissue that connect muscles to bones or other body parts

snare trap

spit a narrow strip of land that juts out into the water

stunted has not grown properly

trinkets jewelry worth very little

Scott O'Dell on Writing

"Writing is hard," Scott O'Dell once said, "harder than digging a ditch, and it requires patience." The most important part of writing, he told people, is to discipline yourself to sit down and do the work.

Most of O'Dell's book ideas came from reading history or biography, or from stories people told him. He always did a lot of research before beginning to write. Often, the research alone would take two or three months. O'Dell loved this part of writing and even said, "Research is what I enjoy most. I often write of events, people, and backgrounds that I know little about, just because I want to know more."

After O'Dell researched a topic completely, he began to write. The process of writing the book usually took him another six months.

O'Dell's daily work habits changed over time. When he first began to write, he wrote all day, from 7 A.M. until 5 P.M., and he typed his work on an electric typewriter. Later, he did most of his writing in the morning, and he wrote with a pen on a yellow pad of paper.

During this latter part of his life, he was already awake and thinking about his writing before dawn. His routine, he once said, was "to lie in bed between sleeping and waking, cultivating my subconscious mind, the mind that we dream with. I go over what I'm going to write that day, not line by line but rather thoroughly."

Between 5 A.M. and 5:30 A.M., O'Dell usually began writing at his desk. He wrote until noon or so. At that time, O'Dell always stopped in the middle of a paragraph that was going well so that it was easy to get right back into his work the next day. Sometimes he went back to writing for a few hours later in the afternoon. But whether he went back to work or not, the story was always on his mind.

O'Dell did a lot of revising as he wrote, often rewriting a paragraph over and over before going on to the next paragraph. After a while he could no longer read what he'd written, and he'd have to start over with a clean sheet of paper.

When he was writing a book, O'Dell became very private, often refusing to see friends or to speak in public. Once or twice a week, he would go out to lunch with his wife, and he would discuss his current project with her.

When he had the time, O'Dell loved meeting his readers and writing to them. He received thousands of letters from children and considered this one of the best parts of his work. He loved children's enthusiasm and honesty, and even appreciated their occasionally critical comments.

For aspiring writers

O'Dell told aspiring writers that the most important part of writing was putting in the time and effort needed to get the writing done. He himself showed a lot of patience and perseverance in his writing life, not only day to day, but over his lifetime. Though he had written seven books for adults before he wrote his first children's book, these books had not received much attention. He was already more than sixty years old when he turned to children's books and his work finally became well known.

O'Dell offered another piece of advice for aspiring writers: Write one quick first draft of the whole book before you begin revising. This was not his method, of course. He revised his work many times before he had a complete manuscript. But O'Dell felt that most people would benefit from writing a complete draft of the piece first. "There is enthusiasm in that first draft," he said.

You Be the Author!

• **Survival story:** Survival stories are exciting to read—and to write. Write one of your own! Imagine that you have been left alone someplace. It could be any isolated spot, from an island to a desert to a mountaintop. Write about one or more of the following:

- What happened? Why were you left alone?
- What do you do now? Figure out the basics: food and water, shelter, clothing.
- What skills and objects do you have that will help you survive? What are you missing that you wish you had?
- What dangers do you face? What are you most afraid of? How will you protect yourself?
- How will you be rescued? What will you do to help make a rescue possible?

• **The Channel Island Indians and the Aleuts:** Karana's tribe was one of the Channel Island Indian tribes, which all shared a similar culture. Find out what is known about these people and write about them. What was everyday life like for other Channel Island Indians? How was their culture similar to that of Karana's tribe? What happened to these tribes?

You can also learn more about the Aleut Indians. The Aleuts originally came from the Aleutian Islands in southwest Alaska. They also had a fascinating culture during the time when *Island of the Blue Dolphins* takes place. Research and write about the Aleuts during the 1800s, when they sailed to the Channel Islands to hunt for sea otters.

• **Animal tale:** Strong feelings often inspire good stories. Write an essay about an animal you have felt strongly about. Your feelings may have been positive or negative—or they may have changed over time, as Karana's feelings for Rontu changed from fear and hate to love. Write about your relationship with an animal from start to finish, making sure the reader understands how you felt about the animal and why, as time passed.

• **Historical fiction:** In historical fiction, an author mixes history and fiction to help us experience what life was like for people in another time and place. Learn more about a historical time and place that interests you. Then, imagine that you were there and write about it. Put yourself right in the middle of the action! For instance, imagine that it is the early 1900s. You and your family have just immigrated to the United States from your farm in another country. Now you are all cooped up together in a small, noisy city tenement building. Where did you come from, and why did you leave? What will you do next? What is the biggest problem your family faces in this new country? How can you help solve it?

Activities

- **Map the island:** Scott O'Dell describes the Island of the Blue Dolphins so vividly that you can draw a map using his descriptions. Try it yourself. See if you can figure out the correct locations for places such as Coral Cove, the headland where Karana builds her house, the village of Ghalas-at, the cave that Karana uses as a second shelter, the place where the Aleuts camp, Black Cave, and Tall Rock.

- **Make a poster of the wildlife:** Many animals live on the Island of the Blue Dolphins or in the nearby ocean. These include wild dogs, red foxes, gray mice, cormorants, red-winged blackbirds, sea otters, blue dolphins, sea elephants, devilfish, whales, starfish, and shellfish. You can find more by looking through the novel. Locate photographs or drawings of these animals. Use what you have gathered or drawings you have created to make a poster of the island's wildlife.

- **Illustrate your favorite scene:** Many of the scenes in the novel would make dramatic drawings, paintings, or dioramas. Illustrate your favorite. Consider such exciting scenes as: the first meeting on the beach between the islanders and the Aleuts, the ship leaving the island as Karana dives into the sea, the dogs circling as Karana sleeps on her rock, Karana paddling out to sea in her canoe, Karana and Rontu trapped in Black Cave, or

Karana in all her finery as she greets the white men who have come to take her from the island.

- **What's in a name?:** Karana's tribe gives each person two names, an everyday name and a special, secret one.

The everyday name describes something about the person. Karana's everyday name is Won-a-pa-lei, which means "The Girl with the Long Black Hair." Pick a new, everyday name for yourself that describes something positive about you.

Each person in Karana's tribe also has a special, secret name that is rarely used, such as Karana and Chowig. What secret name would you choose for yourself? You can also imagine new everyday and special, secret names for everyone in your family or for your closest friends.

- **Make something useful or beautiful or both:** Every object Karana has is made from natural materials. Some of her things are simply useful, such as her spear, and some are beautiful, too, such as her skirt of cormorant feathers and her seashell earrings. Make yourself something useful and possibly beautiful from natural objects. Stick to materials that are clean and dry, such as wood, bark, well-cleaned shells, dried leaves, and stones. You could make something that would help you survive or something that would make your life more comfortable.

- **Discover the wild animals that live near you:** You might be surprised by how many wild animals live near you—even if you live in a large town or city. To find out about them, you can begin by talking with a local librarian, a veterinarian, a parks department wildlife expert, or an animal-shelter assistant. What you do with the information you find is up to you: Use it to make a poster illustrating the local wildlife, write a report for school, or make a booklet to give to your friends. You may be inspired to volunteer with an organization that helps protect wildlife.

• **Read the books that won the Scott O'Dell Award:** Scott O'Dell developed the Scott O'Dell Award for Historical Fiction to encourage people to write and read historical fiction. He wanted to inspire children to be more interested in history, which is so important to understanding the world. Besides that, it's exciting! Read some of the books that won the Scott O'Dell Award, and see if you enjoy historical fiction as much as O'Dell did. You will find a list of these award-winning books in the Related Reading section at the back of this book.

• **Read about Karana in another Scott O'Dell book:** O'Dell wrote a novel called *Zia* because he wanted to explore what happened to Karana after she left the island. The sad truth is that the real Lost Woman of San Nicolas Island died seven weeks after she left the island. Read *Zia* to see how O'Dell imagined those last weeks of Karana's life, in a novel narrated by Karana's fictional niece, Zia.

• **Watch the movie:** *Island of the Blue Dolphins* was made into a movie in 1964. You can buy it or borrow it from the library or video store. As you watch it, think about how the movie is similar to the book and how it is different. Which do you like better, and why?

Other children's books by Scott O'Dell

Alexandra (1984)

The Amethyst Ring (1983)

The Black Pearl (1967)

Black Star, Bright Dawn (1988)

The Captive (1979)

Carlota (1977)

The Castle in the Sea (1983)

Child of Fire (1974)

The Cruise of the Arctic Star (1973)

The Dark Canoe (1968)

The Feathered Serpent (1981)

The Hawk That Dare Not Hunt by Day (1975)

Journey to Jericho (1969)

Kathleen, Please Come Home (1978)

The King's Fifth (1966)

My Name Is Not Angelica (1989)

The Road to Damietta (1985)

Sarah Bishop (1980)

The Serpent Never Sleeps (1987)

Sing Down the Moon (1970)

The Spanish Smile (1982)

Streams to the River, River to the Sea (1986)

Thunder Rolling in the Mountains (with Elizabeth Hall) (1992)
The Treasure of Topo-el-Bampo (1972)
The 290 (1976)
Venus Among the Fishes (with Elizabeth Hall) (1995)
Zia (1976)

Movies
The Black Pearl (1978)
Island of the Blue Dolphins (1964), available on VHS

Survival stories—fiction
Brian's Winter by Gary Paulsen
The Cay by Theodore Taylor
Hatchet by Gary Paulsen
Julie of the Wolves by Jean Craighead George
My Side of the Mountain by Jean Craighead George
Nory Ryan's Song by Patricia Reilly Giff
The Sign of the Beaver by Elizabeth George Speare
  (also an O'Dell Award winner)
Toughboy and Sister by Kirkpatrick Hill

Recipients of the Scott O'Dell Award for Historical Fiction
1984   *The Sign of the Beaver* by Elizabeth George Speare
1985   *The Fighting Ground* by Avi
1986   *Sarah, Plain and Tall* by Patricia MacLachlan
1987   *Streams to the River, River to the Sea* by Scott O'Dell
1988   *Charley Skedaddle* by Patricia Beatty
1989   *The Honorable Prison* by Lyll Becerra de Jenkins
1990   *Shades of Gray* by Carolyn Reeder
1991   *A Time of Trouble* by Pieter Van Raven

1992   *Stepping on the Cracks* by Mary Downing Hahn

1993   *Morning Girl* by Michael Dorris

1994   *Bull Run* by Paul Fleischman

1995   *Under the Blood-Red Sun* by Graham Salisbury

1996   *The Bomb* by Theodore Taylor

1997   *Jip, His Story* by Katherine Patterson

1998   *Out of the Dust* by Karen Hesse

1999   *Forty Acres and Maybe a Mule* by Harriette Robinet

2000   *Two Suns in the Sky* by Miriam Bat-Ami

2001   *The Art of Keeping Cool* by Janet Taylor Lisle

2002   *The Land* by Mildred D. Taylor

Books

Gallo, Donald R., comp. and ed. *Speaking for Ourselves: Autobiographical Sketches by Notable Authors of Books for Young Adults.* Urbana, Ill.: National Council of Teachers of English, 1990.

Harris, Laurie Lanzen, exec. ed. *Biography Today Author Series*, Vol. 2. Detroit, Mich.: Omnigraphics, Inc., 1996.

Heinrichs, Ann. *The California Missions.* Minneapolis, Minn.: Compass Point Books, 2002.

Kingman, Lee, ed. *Newbery and Caldecott Medal Books: 1956–1965.* Boston: Horn Book, 1965.

O'Dell, Scott. *Island of the Blue Dolphins.* Boston: Houghton Mifflin, 1960.

Russell, David L. *Scott O'Dell.* New York: Twayne Publishers, 1999.

Townsend, John Rowe. *A Sense of Story: Essays on Contemporary Writers for Children.* Philadelphia: Lippincott, 1971.

Newspapers and magazines

The ALAN Review, Winter 1999, Volume 26, Number 2, pp. 14–21.

The Los Angeles Times, Los Angeles, Calif., Dec. 13, 1990, p. 10.

The Los Angeles Times, Los Angeles, Calif., Mar. 18, 2001, p. B3.

The New York Times Book Review, New York, N.Y., March 27, 1960, pp. 40–41.

The New York Times, New York, N.Y., April 15, 1984, p. WC 27.

Videocassette

A Visit with Scott O'Dell, Houghton Mifflin Author and Artist Series, 13 min., Boston: Houghton Mifflin, 1983, videocassette.

Web sites

Scott O'Dell Web Page:
  www.scottodell.com
Internet School Library Media Center:
  falcon.jmu.edu/~ramseyil/odell.htm
Santa Barbara Museum of Natural History:
  www.sbnature.org/chumash/lowom.htm